# ACKNOWLEDGMENTS

We would like to dedicate this book to our parents, **Al & Elena Kipple** and **Tom & Diana Wherry**. Thanks for putting up with us for all those years; we love you. Oh, and Mom: In college I didn't break that kid's computer playing Nerf basketball; I got drunk and angry and threw it against a wall…sorry, my bad.

Special thanks to Brett Fullmer for believing in our idea and giving us the support and guidance to keep our site up and running. Thanks to Patty Souza and Leslie Black for all the work they do. Thanks to Alison Fargis for thinking we could take this website and put it on paper for the world. Thank you to Peter Lynch and Sourcebooks for taking a risk on us and dealing with three inexperienced authors and making us feel like we were John Grisham. Thanks to Alec Miller for his counsel. Thanks to all our friends and family, specifically Joe Scarpo for all his help, advice, and guidance.

Adam would like to thank the teachers (you know who you are) who helped him hone his talents to become who he is today, and tell all those teachers who told him he wouldn't do anything with his life to kiss his ass!

A very special NON-thanks to Luis Muniz, Frank Scholer, William Reilly McClure, Anthony Pecora, Chris Wojton, Brandon Herman, Joe Dagher, Tom Polley, Aaron Lim, Kevin Coleman, Michael Sandor, Joe Teevan, Thomas McComas, Brain Bausch, Paul Interdonato, Michael Gillott, Brian Fox, Alex Razavi, Jack Sullivan, Brandon Evans, and Clint Wherry. We hate you all.

Most importantly, we would like to thank our FANS! You guys are the best. We appreciate your dedication, submissions, comments, stories, and everything else you guys do. If it weren't for all of you, we wouldn't be here. As long as you guys continue to keep up all the great work you do, we will continue to provide you with a few laughs and an escape from your day! THANK YOU!

# DISCLAIMER

We are in *no* way affiliated or associated with Walmart. We also personally have nothing against Walmart. We, along with most of America, shop at Walmart for nearly everything we need. This book and our website are simply satirical social commentary about the extraordinary sights found at America's favorite store. Walmart is Americana, baby!

All photographs and stories have been submitted by the users of www.PeopleofWalmart.com, the rights to which have been granted to ALA Design, LLC. Since we do not take the photographs ourselves, and many are taken with cell phone cameras, some of the pictures are not of the highest quality and may appear blurry and/or out of focus. So don't look at a picture and think you are losing your sight; it's just somebody's hand shaking excitedly as they run down the aisle with their camera phone.

**WARNING:** Some of the pictures and stories contained in this book are very graphic. We are not responsible if after reading a story or looking at a picture you have the sudden urge to vomit, stab yourself in the eye, stab a nearby co-worker or friend, jump out a window, drink bleach, bathe in bleach, clean your eyes with bleach, quit your job and spend the rest of your life in a secluded cave, cut off a limb, become aroused (Really? That's sick!), rally people for a book burning, divorce your partner, skydive without a parachute, join the Taliban, or sell all your assets and give the money to us (actually, that last one is fine). So pretty much, continue reading at your own risk.

# INTRODUCTION

Let's face it: We all have seen the people who obviously don't have mirrors, or at least family and friends to lock them in a basement. And for some reason, they all seem to congregate at Walmart.

It's not everywhere that you can shop for milk at 10 a.m. next to a 400-pound mother of six wearing a pink tube top, leopard tights, and hooker heels. Where else can one go to pick up underwear at 3 o'clock in the afternoon and spot the greatest mullet of all time? And that same guy has not only a supreme mullet, but is wearing a mustard-stained wife beater (which only accents his extreme amount of body hair) and camo pants. And yet, amazingly, it's also the same place you might bump into your favorite actor, actress, musician, or thoroughly undeserved famous-for-no-reason reality star. You never know whom you will encounter, but you know you'll never forget it.

PeopleofWalmart.com was founded in August 2009 by three friends after an inspirational trip to Walmart. It was another beautiful, sunny day in Myrtle Beach, and our town was buzzing about the new Walmart located just 10 miles north of, well, another Walmart. Okay, the town wasn't buzzing, but there was definitely a new Walmart right by an old one, and we needed groceries, so off to the new store we went to check it out.

As the three of us perused the aisles, filling our carts with moon pies, oatmeal pies, and some delicious Walmart-brand blueberry muffin cereal (seriously, it's awesome), we came across an older man. He was wearing what I have to assume are the world-record-setting shortest jean shorts and a tattered tank top that was only visible from the back or side due to his salt-and-pepper ZZ Top beard. After a few subtle looks and a quick laugh among ourselves, it was off to the frozen food section for Hot Pockets and frozen taquitos.

It was there, in that frozen food section of the brand-new Walmart, that we found our muse. She was what you could conservatively refer to as a "robust" woman. Now I'm not a scale, but if I was forced to offer a guess I'd feel safe saying 350-plus pounds (and that's using *Price Is Right* rules of course). And that's okay; there's nothing wrong with being overweight. This is America; it's what we do. However, what's not good is accompanying that full-figured body with full-on hooker gear. Our awe at her getup started at the bottom, with her gold high-heeled shoes accompanied by that stripper wrap that goes up the leg. After that came pink fishnet stockings that looked like they were cutting through mashed potatoes. Thankfully, her 4-inch skirt was positioned in the right place so as not to give us nightmares. Unfortunately, her tube-top didn't cover quite as much as the mannequin in the store probably showed. And of course, just in case this fine lady didn't catch our attention on her own, she accessorized her outfit with a four-year-old kid running around like a banshee on one of those sweet kid leashes disguised as a monkey backpack.

On our way back home, we reflected on a profound observation of "no matter what state, what town, or what time of day it is, you will always see someone or something crazy at Walmart." The lightbulb went off. We got home, unloaded our groceries, bought the domain name, and had the site designed by the next day.

The rest is…well the rest is that a year later, we've seen thousands of the most bizarre and hilarious photos and received everything ranging from marriage proposals to death threats and even a picture of a naked woman straddling a 6-foot stuffed monkey. And to think, now you are sitting on the toilet reading this book, based on a crazy idea by three friends. Enjoy!

–Adam Kipple, Andrew Kipple, Luke Wherry

# RAISING SOME EYEBROWS

I like talking to her because she always seems so surprised and interested in what I'm saying. That, and because she kinda looks like the old lady in Adam Sandler's *Eight Crazy Nights*.

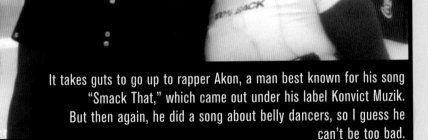

It takes guts to go up to rapper Akon, a man best known for his song "Smack That," which came out under his label Konvict Muzik. But then again, he did a song about belly dancers, so I guess he can't be too bad.

## PICNIC TIME FOR TEDDY BEARS

Custom-made, cute, cuddly little teddy bear earmuffs are the *cutest* thing in the world…when you're six.

## COMPLETE WITH HANDLEBARS

Put your finger down; you're embarrassing yourself in front of mustache greatness. Would you try to flex in a picture with Schwarzenegger circa 1975?

FLORIDA

Are you kidding me? I will pay you anything you want for that jacket! The single biggest regret in my life is that awful day when I threw away my Reba McEntire jean jacket after discovering she wasn't going to be in *Tremors 2*.

## SKUNKED

Skunk head? Really? As if wearing a dead animal pelt on your head Davy Crockett-style wasn't enough, you decided to go with a classy animal such as a skunk to flop on your head.

6

PENNSYLVANIA

## CAR TROUBLE

There is no joke to this. You drove a f*cking car through a store.

## A PERFECT MATCH

All I'm saying is if those shoes aren't sold exclusively with that hat, I simply cannot comprehend your dedication to matching. Yet I still love it.

## THE TWILIGHT PRINCESS

Honestly, if you're that excited for the new Zelda game (which by the way you shouldn't be this excited for anything) please buy it and go home instead of scaring all the children trying to play games while their parents shop.

## SLEEP IT OFF

You laugh, but this guy is a genius and an innovator for all men. What do you think the odds are that his wife insists on dragging him shopping with her ever again?

# UNIQUE AND DIFFERENT

You literally cannot prove any further that every snowflake is completely different from the others!

## BIRD FEEDER

"This bird loves me!"–Yes it does, but only because that fe-mullet is a mobile nest with what I assume is an unlimited supply of insects to feast on.

## PET YOUR MEAT!

So many questions instantly come to mind. First, who decides which goat gets to go home with Little Billy and which goat gets to go with Chef Billy? Second, what is your reaction if I wanted both?

## GROWING UP IS HARD TO DO

For argument's sake, let's say I concede the crazy assumption that it's okay for your child to ride *under* the shopping cart. Don't you think it's time to stop once your kid is protruding from it on all sides, let alone old enough to vote?

## PUMPKIN PATCHES

An accurate representation of the inside—nothing but pumpkin seeds and slimy gooey stuff.

## REBEL WITHOUT A CAUSE

I guess sometimes you just can't shake that inner fifteen-year-old rebellious girl who's trapped inside.

Just in case you were under the impression that he was not gangster he spelled it out for you. And also labeled where he might put his guns. (And maybe "$7" is stitched into his other pocket.)

## A REAL SWEETHEART

Check out how sweet the hearts and flannel look together! I am amazed Armani hasn't jumped on this yet to make a suit.

...and while you were reading *this*, I threw up in my mouth.

# WHAT'S THE OPPOSITE OF "BAD ASS"?

"Bad Ass Boys Drive Bad Ass Pontiacs"? First, there is no such thing as a bad-ass Pontiac. Second, tell me where you got that shirt custom made so I can go smack them in the face. Someone should be responsible for that transaction.

# COOKIE MONSTER

At the moment, I am working at a Subway in a Walmart.

I had a customer come in one day and everything started out smoothly. This lady had been coming in for quite some time, so I kind of recognized her. She's overweight, looking like trailer trash and riding (as we call them in our store) a fat cart. She orders a foot-long tuna sandwich and wants us to put all the veggies on it.

Everything was going smoothly until the veggies were placed on the sandwich. That's when she said to me, "This may be a strange request." At this point, I'm thinking that I've heard many people say that, and the requests are never really that strange. So I ask her what she wants. And she proceeded to ask me to put four white macadamia nut cookies on her tuna sandwich.

I think I gave her a really disgusted look, but I'm not sure. I obliged and placed the cookies on her sandwich. But she wasn't done yet. She then asked me to cover the cookies with vinegar until they were soggy and ready to fall apart. Then to top it off, she made me double up on the mayo over the soggy cookies.

At this point, I felt like I wanted to puke all over her sandwich. I think I may have a little in the back of my throat.

This lady is now a regular customer and she gets this same thing every day.

## HEAD-ON COLLISION

I was going to yell at him about the little girl's safety, but it looks like she has a great airbag so I let it slide.

**BEEP BEEP!**

I don't have the heart to tell him I saw the Roadrunner leave hours ago.

## BABY GOT BACK...BOOBS

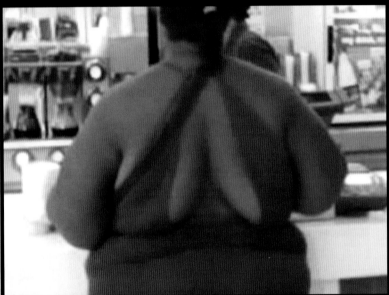

You kind of want to just pull one of those straps aside just to prove you're actually seeing what you think you're seeing. Although you might be happier to find out she's got some sort of Exorcist thing going on!

I'm gonna go out on a limb here and assume you feel as if you're the lone white horse in that little gem you stitched on the back of your jean shirt.

## ORANGE YOU GLAD YOU CAN SEE ME?

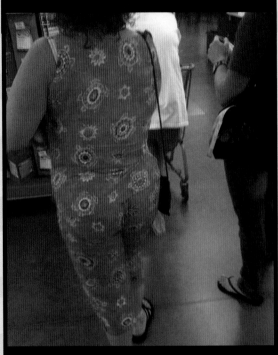

No, it's cool; I like feeling like I'm living in an acid trip while I shop. Thanks!

COLORADO

## SOMETHING SEEMS FISHY...

How is it that you remembered to put on your calf fishnets but forgot to cover the booty?

## SWISS MISS

She looks like a life-size hot chocolate with marshmallows!
Drink it in!

UNKNOWN

Oh, it's like an awful-flavored lollipop! I don't want any of that.

# GREEN MAN!

Not all of us have the luxury of owning a Wii, especially when you're so busy carrying objects across green screens and/or dancing at sporting events!

## DASHED FUTURE

Way to leave something to the imagination...like how you will ever get a job.

# A WHITE WEDDING

Well it's nice to see the dowry is making a comeback. Socks, meat, and jarred cheese might not be a lot, but it's a start.

## LOOKING FOR A CLEAN BREAK

It kinda looks like a giant turd is just slowly creeping its way out and attacking her head.

# KING OF HEARTS

Suicide King, take a hint. Sorry, I mean you're an Ace-hole. I mean you're one Jack-off. Wait, I mean nice bedazzle work; could you really be Straight? I mean, you should take that jacket and Royal Flush it down the toilet...Yep, that was it.

## ALMOND JOY-LESS

I guess she feels like a nut!!!

## I WANT YOU!

Sure, I could make a joke at the improper shopping attire. OR I could point out the fact that the person who is blatantly pointing at the barely covered booty is also holding a picture of Uncle Sam, who is also pointing at the barely covered booty...

TEXAS

Let him go; nobody wanted to tell him what "doggie-style" actually is, so he's harmless.

## HEAVY FLOW

Well to be fair, it is called a men-struation cycle, so I can see the cause for confusion.

# COWBOY MEETS COWGIRL

I don't care that he is dressed like that; I'm just saying next time he asks me to go shoe shopping with him, he better toss on a pair of panties!

## REALITY CHECK

Well obviously I deserved that for walking around thinking
I was a real somebody. What a gut check! Thanks guy
with neck tattoo for helping me finally see that.

WASHINGTON

## IN NEED OF A JOB

I'm here about the Blow Job

I'm not really sure that's the type of job opening they have. If I'm wrong, then I too would also like to inquire about that.

# FOREIGNER POLICY

This guy lived his dream of meeting the band that made him a "Juke Box Hero."

PENNSYLVANIA

# YOU'RE NEXT

I have always heard of the horrendous third-party parenting that goes on in Texas. Even though I've lived here for twenty-five years, it took me six years after having a child to discover it firsthand. And man, some people are a little too bold.

I decided to take my four- and six-year-olds with me to Walmart one day to pick up a few drinks and chips that I couldn't seem to find at any other store in town. We had already been to a few other stores where my wife and I usually do our shopping. So, as you can imagine, their short attention spans were running on empty. That, and my wife and I were a little agitated from dealing with the atypical Dallas hustle and bustle.

I'm a man, so after four hours of shopping, my mind and temperament was sketchy at best. But on this day I was borderlining insanity. It just so happens that my six-year-old decides he wants to get a little testy after passing the toy aisle. After putting him in check with a stern warning for his partial temper-tantrum, he settles down.

Now for those of you who have more than one child, you're all too familiar with the common fact that trouble usually comes in pairs. Especially when one child is two years older than the other and knows how to manipulate. So without fail, our four-year-old tries her hand when I split from the rest of my family to grab the drinks. My daughter starts throwing one hell of a fit that I hear four aisles down. A matter of fact, I dropped the drinks because it scared the shit out of me. Now when it comes to my daughter, she's a little more complicated, because she can sense my anxiety with spanking her in public and tends to capitalize on our father-daughter relationship–or as my wife calls it, Sucker Syndrome. I've never had a problem with disciplining my son; it always was second nature for him and I to have a mutual agreement: the paddle. But since my daughter is rather petite like my wife, disciplining her is always a bit awkward for me. That, and the fact that my hand dwarves her little behind. (For me, it's like trying to spank a grapefruit.) And of course, she knows this and works that angle. I felt a little bad, as all parental senses were tingling and screaming "ass-whooping."

But I carefully took a moment to assess my options. It was in this moment that I realized it was apparent that my wife and daughter had some telepathic connection, because I could sense the rapidly narrowing proximity of my wife by the "oh sh*t" look on my daughter's face. Inevitably it seems my wife had enough and decided to deliver a swift punishment. So commenced the spanking in Aisle 3.

Now it wasn't but maybe three licks into it that a woman and her boyfriend, both in their early twenties, stopped to gander upon my child's disposition. Now for a brief moment, even they had the common sense not to interrupt my wife as she exercised her parental right. Matter of fact. With the exception of her counting joyously and the slight uncanny resemblance to a jilted dominatrix and the Count from *Sesame Street*,

I was quite proud of her. But I wasn't prepared for what was about to be blurted out of this woman's mouth. As my wife sat my daughter back in the basket and reprimanded her for the way she had acted, this woman decides to interject and voice her opinion on how my wife should have handled the situation.

She turns to my wife and says, "What is wrong with you!?"

My wife, befuddled with the question, replies, "Excuse me?"

"You can't do that!" the woman said. "That's public humiliation."

I turned and looked at my wife, and for a brief moment I could actually see the gears in her head stop. And what sounded like a monster truck roaring out of control emerged.

My wife then replied by informing the woman, "If I had wanted your opinion, I would have asked for it."

The woman then replied, "Well, you shouldn't be spanking your child like that in public."

Now at this point I began to get a little agitated. I was still a bit befuddled at this woman's audacity and her boyfriend laughing about it. Well, needless to say I lost my anger and informed both the woman and her boyfriend where they could kindly "shove their opinions." I then turned to the woman and told her, "I really don't give a sh*t what you think, as it's apparent that you could have used some discipline yourself. So kindly take yourself and your giggling boyfriend there and move along, before I do what your daddy should have done!" I've never seen someone's jaw drop that far. And I would have kept a straight face if it hadn't been for my son who conveniently chimed in, "Daddy, you want my belt?" Score one for parental rights, including discipline.

## GRINDIN' THAT POLE

For $30 for 3 1/2 minutes, I probably would too.

# WEDDING BELLS ARE RINGING

She has the most romantic cousin in the world...

Ehhhh, I'm not impressed. You can take that certification class for free online...

# ON THE OUTSIDE LOOKING IN

He stands there every night, but nobody is really worried because he still hasn't figured out how to actually go into the store.

The weird part is that although my Gaydar is going off the charts, I know all the wives and girlfriends out there still don't see it and aren't convinced.

## PUTTIN' OUT THE VIBE

What are the chances of finding shorts to match that shirt? What are the chances of finding a girl to talk to a guy who found shorts to match that shirt?

## WE DON'T WANT TO GET TOO FORMAL

"These keys looked bigger when I tried them on."

## YOU BUTTON-HOOKED ME

Just a goat shopping at Walmart...I don't see what's so funny.

ARIZONA

## YOU LOOKING AT SOMETHIN'?

How cute and cuddly are those stuffed...OH MY GOD!

**NO TAN LINE!**

Is it even legal to look this good?

**PINK BELLY**

Britney Spears let herself go...again.

## THIS IS WHY AMERICA IS THE GREATEST PLACE ON EARTH

Yes, you see that correctly. It is an old man with big, supple, delicious-looking breast implants.

**BEAT DRUMS! BEAT DRUMS!**

Now all we need is Dr. Teeth and the Electric Mayhem for a reunion tour.

**SERIOUSLY, GUYS—IT'S AN INDIAN SYMBOL FOR GOOD FORTUNE**

How could you ever, ever, ever ever ever, E.V.E.R. think this is appropriate to wear in public? WOW!

A motorcycle, huh? I guess your Buick got damaged while you were bench-pressing it.

# TOUGH TO SEE PAST ALL THIS AWESOMENESS

Wouldn't you like to know what I plan on doing with this beer and olive oil?

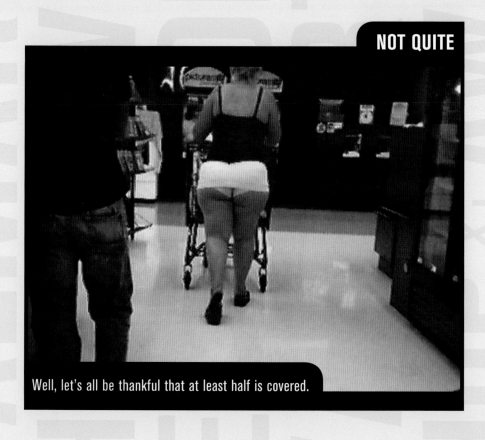

Well, let's all be thankful that at least half is covered.

# HOW DO YOU LIKE IT?

I am speechless.

UTAH

OH...MY...GOD!!!

There should be an application process in order to procreate.

## LIL' BOW WOW

Parents, STOP THIS! Stop this now! Your kid is not a dog; get him off the leash. I don't want to hear that you are too busy to watch your child in public. Your priorities are kid first, remembering milk second.

NORTH CAROLINA

# BROUGHT TO YOU BY A WAL-CREATURE

I was in Walmart two days before Christmas last year. I happened to be nearly nine months pregnant and had feet, among other body parts, the size of balloons, so I was obviously insane to go into Walmart. But I had to buy two things, and one of them (specific ribbon for my nursery's wall letters) could only be found at Walmart. So off I went through the torrential crowds. Having snagged my two items, I headed to the express lane, where, as usual, the twenty items or less guideline was being ignored by people with carts piled high with items. I decided to stand my ground though, as the lines were no better anywhere else. When I was two people from the register, I noticed a girl about sixteen years old standing to the right of me, examining the bags of chips that were displayed there. She picked up a bag of Doritos, decided to purchase them, and then stepped in front of me and stood there. I kind of stared at her, totally blown away that she had just cut in line so confidently. I turned around and looked at the woman behind me who shrugged her shoulders, equally confused. I tapped the girl on the shoulder. When she turned around, I said, "Um…you just cut in front of me?" She looked at me, seemingly not understanding why I had dared to speak to her, then shrugged and said, "I only have this one thing" and turned around. Mainly due to exhaustion, I kept my mouth shut. However, once over the shock, I realized what I should have said, which was, "I don't give a $%^^&& you little ^&*(. If you have one item or 422, you can walk your little %^&*( to the back of the line!"

Somebody come here and pick up my jaw; I can't seem to find it now that my eyes popped out of my head.

## NEED MORE SUPPLIES

Have I been huffing what? Huffing paint? What? Really? Where would you get that?...What if I did? It would only make the cat food taste better.

**TIGHTER!!!**

This guy kind of looks like a big condom (but I don't have the balls to tell him that).

**FRONT TO BACK**

Now that's a titty!

# WHO WEARS SHORT SHORTS?

I didn't even know they could make shirts that bright.

## RISKY BUSINESS

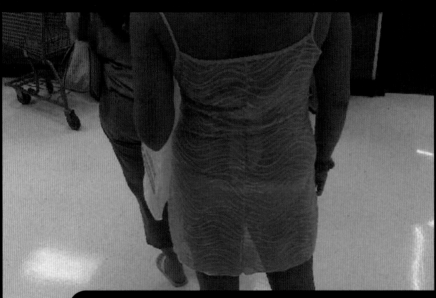

I think she is returning the chocolate syrup for whipped cream and strawberries. You don't want to grow out of that lingerie.

## CRACKIN' JOKES

I guess he is just setting me up to "crack a joke," huh?
Editor's Note: Although not hilarious, we thought this
might be in better taste than a "crack baby" joke.

# I CAN TRANSFORM YA

It looks like someone snapped this picture in the middle
of her transformation into the fifty-foot woman.

ARIZONA

## PICTURE ME ROLLIN'

I hate to break it to everyone, but I don't think the waistline on those shorts was rolled up by hand.

# GANG GREEN

"'Crushing all deceivers/ smashing nonbelievers/ never-ending potency' Oooh, Mom, can we get Cheetos?"

## OLD YELLER

His family doesn't have a dog, they just give him a big ladle and that bag of Ol' Roy lasts him a good couple of days.

**WHEN YOU GET THE POWER, THEN YOU GET THIS WOMAN**

No! No! No, I would not like to say hello to your little friend.

## DUELING BANJOS

I didn't know Deliverance had a his-and-her section.

## OH NO!

Let's all try to think of a scenario where this doesn't end badly...Yeah, I'm stumped too.

CANADA

## CHICKEN AND THE EGG

The ultimate question: Did the mullet come with the sweatshirt or did she receive the sweatshirt when she got the haircut?

## A LOW GROWL

I doubt this Tiger's wife is worried about extramarital affairs.

UNKNOWN

## SURRENDER THE CHIPS AND COOKIES AND PRETZELS AND DIGNITY

Listen vending machine, don't try to be a hero. Just give her everything you got and maybe we can all walk away from this unharmed.

## CLOUD OF DIRT

After all these years I really thought Pig-Pen would have cleaned himself up and tried to get out from under Charlie Brown's shadow...

## WHAT'S UP DOC?

Sometimes she just likes to go to the store and hide out in the produce department waiting for someone to mistake her for a carrot. No one ever does, but she really enjoys it, and we don't have the heart to tell her she's wasting her time.

# PARTY IN THE BACK

We are just proud she finally managed to not wear it backward for once.

# YOU KNOW YOU WANT ME

I was in our local Walmart today with my mother and my twelve-year-old daughter. We were all very tired from our spring break outing and were in the store picking up a few needed items. It was early in the afternoon on a Friday, and the store was very busy. A "lady" (and I use that term loosely) in her early twenties with tri-colored pink, black, and purple hair was behind me with a cart. She hit the back of my foot three times with her cart.

After the third time I turned around and said, "Excuse me."

She replied, "If your fat ass would walk a little faster I wouldn't have to keep hitting you." We exchanged some very colorful words that then ended in me saying "bite me." By now we had drawn a crowd.

Her reply to my "bite me" comment was, "You are more than a mouthful."

I then turned to her, stuck out my chest, ran my hand firmly across my breast, and said, "Oh baby you know you want me and you would love every minute of it, just admit it." My mother disappeared into a different aisle in the store and my twelve-year-old hung her head in shame.

LOVE IT, LOVE IT. Note: I am a BBW and proud of it.

## HAWK AND ANIMAL

Home Theater

Is this like a "hook 'em while they're young," but for unemployment?

## COOKING BY THE BOOK

Is this Walmart located in LazyTown or something? Is it odd that I am a male in my midtwenties and I know about the kids' show *LazyTown*? Well, mind your business and just laugh at the goofy girls in wigs.

## TUCKIN' IT IN

It might be time to discover a pair of scissors when you have to start tucking your hair into your pocket so people don't step on it.

HAWAII

## THROUGH THE FIRE AND FLAMES

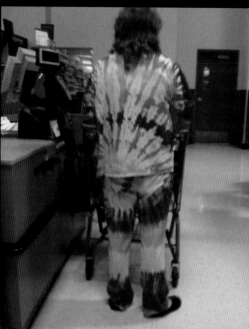

When I recover from my current seizure, someone please remind me to set those clothes on fire, whether she is in them or not.

## CRACK KILLA

New rule: If we can see your butt crack, we are allowed to draw on it to make some sort of funny face, so everyone else can at least chuckle to themselves when they're subject to looking at your business.

ARKANSAS

## THE STEEL CURTAIN

As Steelers fans, we know all about Steelers Country and Steelers Nation. However, we are also in favor of some sort of jurisdictional boundaries. This isn't Heinz Field.

# OH CAPTAIN, MY CAPTAIN

Captain Planet looked the par; Captain America was decked out in his red, white, and blue; Captain Morgan is a pirate and pirates love rum; hell, even Captain Crunch did his thing…but for some reason I just can't believe he would be *THE* Captain Love.

TEXAS

We like to still dress identical so people can tell we are twins.

# BABY MAMA

To all the pregnant ladies out there: Do not put
your baby's clothing on while it's still in the womb.

UNKNOWN

## DOUBLE BREASTED

When your other boobs are covering the material holding up your boobs, it's time to think about a T-shirt.

# LADY GAG GAG

Why even wear pants at all?

How do you know your day is going to shit? The best decision you've made thus far is putting on a fanny pack.

## RESPONSE FOR EVERYTHING

What types of things are you involved in that it becomes more convenient to just tattoo "Fuck You" on your arm than to flip someone off or actually exert all that energy to say it?

ARIZONA

## EASY RIDER

Life would be so much better if this guy rides a Harley! Now, if I was a betting man, I would say it's more likely to be a pink Vespa scooter, but then again in my line of work I've seen stranger things...Like a guy with a pink purse, white boots, and a helmet on.

## SWING LOW, SWEET CHARIOT

I guess just like regular **boobs**, even back boobs get saggy with age.

UNKNOWN

# MONKEY SEE, MONKEY DO

Sure, it's adorable when they do that and then eat the bananas the workers give them, but you weren't there when they got scared by the PA system and started throwing their poop all over the place.

## WASTIN' AWAY

The custom-cut 1980s-style collar done to
show off the tats...well played.

GEORGIA

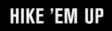

## HIKE 'EM UP

I've heard of running shorts, but that's just ridiculous.

## ALONG FOR THE RIDE

What she doesn't know won't hurt her...

OKLAHOMA

They say a picture is worth a thousand words. And yet I'm speechless.

# IN THE FLESH

I remember several years back when I was working for a local Walmart store. One day we had a customer who decided to enlighten us with the news of the second coming of Jesus.

The woman was maybe in her forties. She did not seem to be intoxicated and actually acted like she was levelheaded and thinking on her own…in the beginning.

She walked into the store, stood in front of the registers, and proceeded to shout, "Jesus Christ sent me here with a message. He will be returning to the earth to take the saved to Heaven." She even gave us a date when this event would happen.

All of us cashiers just returned to work. About fifteen minutes later the woman returned to the front of the store to repeat her message. In her short absence, the woman had stripped down to her birthday suit so that she could deliver the message just how the good Lord had sent her into this world.

If I was forced to take a guess at what she does for a living, I would probably go with Michael Jackson's fairy godmother.

# NORSE PRINCESS WAS TAKEN

You can find more pictures on her eHarmony profile page Viking_Queen.

# COCK-A-DOODLE-DON'T

I guess you're allowed to be a little cocky when you're the only one in your trailer park who knows how to spell "redneck."

ALABAMA

# A HAT TO MATCH

He dressed up his onesie with a cool orange wig. She accented her onesie with a cute pink hat. Mom, way to slack off and accent your onesie with a depressing hoodie. Just because you're dressed in sleepwear doesn't mean you have to be lazy.

## MATCH MADE IN WALMART

Still don't believe in true love?

## WORK OF ART

Once you stop laughing, take the time to really appreciate the aesthetics of this mullet. As far as mullets go, this thing is extremely well kept—no split ends, seamless transition from business to party, no grease! It really is a work of art.

## I WANNA BE BAD

Bad girl, huh? Were you a bootlegger during Prohibition or something?

## HE'D LIKE TO WELCOME YOU TO MUNCHKIN LAND

Oh come on! There was no Angel Soft in Munchkin Land!

UNKNOWN

I would have LOVED to hear his wedding vows!

# WHAT A COCK

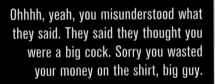

Ohhhh, yeah, you misunderstood what they said. They said they thought you were a big cock. Sorry you wasted your money on the shirt, big guy.

KANSAS

## ROLLIN' DOWN THE STREET

It's Snoopy D-O-Double Gizzle stoppin' by the Wal for some juice to go with that gin.

## HOT DIGGITY DOG

On a scale of 1 to 10, where do you think his level of giving a f*ck is? What I'm feeling right now is straight jealousy for that dude.

## PUSS IN BOOTS

No, Gertrude, I can't think of a single reason why you are having trouble finding a date for Saturday nights.

## WHO FLUNG POO?

She is probably trying to convince a nice elderly woman that the little ball of sh*t that was thrown at her face must have come from some other monkey, because little Kiki wouldn't do such a thing.

OKLAHOMA

When you know you got it, you can't even try hiding it. It's as if a golden retriever were transformed into a glorious man!

## ANGRY BEAVER

Ummm...you look like a beaver! There is no joke accompanying this at all. Your big, weird, creepy hair makes you look like a beaver.

UNKNOWN

## LOTS OF TAIL

It's not her fault; that guy's fabulous rat tail makes all the girls pull their skirts up.

"Hey, PoWM, this is probably staged to get in your book!"
Well if this guy grew that enchanting ponytail for eleven years so he could one day squeeze into his tightest shirt, Lt. Dangle shorts, and goth boots for the purpose of taking a picture at Walmart and getting his fifteen minutes of fame on our website...then I guess he got one over on us.

## THE QUICKER PICKER-UPPER

You already picked up as much dirt and dust off the floor with your feet as you could, son, so it's time to start the full body sweep now.

# AWKWARD...

Ok, so I was at Walmart with a couple of my friends and we were in the bathroom. We're talking between the stalls like girls do, and we hear this voice: "Girls, can you help me?" I came out of the stall and, while washing my hands, asked what the problem was. The lady in the end stall says, "I need help. I went to the bathroom and now I need help. Can you give me some paper towels with warm water and soap?" As I'm getting the paper towels for her, I hear the stall door open. Yep. There she stands, pants around her ankles, shirt up over the boobs. My friends and I were in shock!

I tried to hand her the paper towels so I could get the heck out of there, but she says, "No, I need *you* to wipe it." I was a premed student at the time, so I was trying to be levelheaded and calm. I explained to the lady that I could not do that for her, that it was unsafe for her *and* for me. She didn't get it. She simply said that she couldn't reach and needed help. (She was a bigger woman, in case you haven't guessed.)

By this time a clerk came in and the woman asked *her* to do it. The clerk said that her job description did not include wiping asses. Then we tried to locate her family members, but she said they had dropped her off and were coming back to pick her up later. Once we convinced her that we were *not* going to wipe her ass, she just said, "Well can you check to see if I got it all?" She then proceeded to turn around to show us her ass. At this point, we were done and walked out without looking back. Unbelievable!

# THE WALMART CRIB: BLACK FRIDAY EDITION

This is absolutely ridiculous. How stupid and reckless could someone possibly be? There really needs to be some sort of parenting test that you have to pass.

**IT FEELS LIKE A MIDGET IS HANGING FROM MY NECKLACE**

I'm not a mother, but I'm pretty sure there are more appropriate ways to breast feed than just letting your kid swing from your tit while you push your cart up and down the aisles looking for lampshades.

## NO PANTS DANCE

At what point does a person just say, "F*ck it, I don't need to put on shoes or pants"?

GEORGIA

**133**

# CUPID MAKES 'EM QUIVER

Who had a better Valentine's Day than you? The four to seven women who are loyal to Willy the Pimp, that's who.

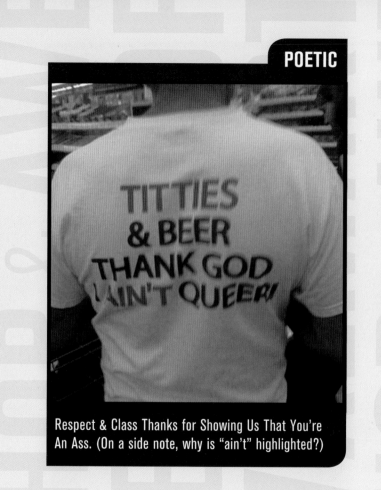

Respect & Class Thanks for Showing Us That You're An Ass. (On a side note, why is "ain't" highlighted?)

# THANK YOU?

Probably the only way you get any, huh? Also, I notice there is a paw print, so does that mean you want to make love to an animal's corpse? I'm not sure which would disturb me more.

I passed out from the amount of obvious jokes that instantly rushed to my brain.

## TELL US HOW YOU REALLY FEEL

What type of incident has to go down for you to get motivated enough to go out and get a custom shirt with "I Hate Queers" written on it?

## THE IRONY OF "SELF-CHECKOUT"

Hey, Beyoncé, throw on some pants and a whole shirt...your gut is creeping into the bags.

FULL MOON

Hiring Center
APPLY NOW!

Mike Rowe wouldn't even scope out that job!

UNKNOWN

Why do I have a feeling Jim Henson is behind her working her arms?

# SMART THINKING

You may say this guy is crazy for wearing that outfit.
I say he is crazy smart for wearing that bright orange
hat so hunters know he's not a real leopard.
(But I also say he is crazy for wearing that outfit.)

INDIANA

## DREADFUL PLEASURES

You ever catch yourself looking at some tacky sh*t a store is selling and think, "How high would someone have to be to buy this junk?" Maybe this guy has the answer.

# THE ANGRY BEAVER

Why would you do that? For a sense of security? It's like you are being spooned 24-7.

Even as these species are becoming extinct, scientists are still trying to determine whether rat tails are a dominant or recessive gene.

# MASTER CHIEF

To all the girlfriends out there who complain that their boyfriends spend more time playing Halo than they do with them, quit b\*tching and be happy this guy isn't your boyfriend.

PENNSYLVANIA

## TOO MUCH JUNK

Who put the shorts on that baby elephant?
Hahahaha! Animals in clothing–that is classic!

## BUNNY LOVE

A Playboy bunny tattoo? I hate to be the bearer of bad news, but I doubt scraping rabbit off the road for dinner will get you noticed by Hugh Hefner.

# NOT YOUR AVERAGE SONG AND DANCE

Unfortunately the associate at Dutch Boy paint company who had this "great new marketing idea" was let go and could not be reached for comment.

## CAT WOMAN

A girl painted like a cat buying cat food. My guess is she ends up happily married with three kids and a white picket fence. Maybe only two kids, but definitely not sad and alone surrounded by forty-six cats while she watches the weather channel all day and yells to her neighbors that the government is spying on her.

## AN IMPOSTER

Remember, kids: He is not really Santa, so DO NOT try to sit on his lap.

# BROTHERLY LOVE

Brothers tend to do embarrassing things to each other on a regular basis; I remember several occasions of flooring, wedgies, ghost pushes, and whatnot occurring at the Mart, mostly happening to my younger brother, much to his lament. Little did I know he had diabolical revenge planned.

It started when he slipped me some crushed-up ex-lax–type pills in my sandwich before the weekly Walmart trip. I had no idea anything was amiss till we were cruising the electronics section and I felt the hand of nature reach out and grip my bowels with tremendous force. He must have seen the look on my face as I started booking to the bathroom because he followed to enjoy the product of his treachery.

I didn't make it all the way–maybe three-quarters of the way–before there was a presence in my shorts, which sped up my run and increased the area affected. Once in the restroom I raced to a stall (thankfully they were all empty). Moments later I hear the door open and my brother's maniacal laughter rang through the small room as my guts poured out. Needless to say, I began to swear my own revenge and call him every name I could think of.

A few minutes passed, and I was feeling slightly better–enough to begin to think about cleaning myself up, which I would need help with. I began to yell at him to bring me a warm wet paper towel with soap and a second one without soap and a third dry one. No response. I began to get really upset. I demanded finally: "Get me the fucking towels now or you fucking die no joke your throat will be in my hands; I have nothing to lose I'm covered in shit and I'll come out of this stall and kick your ass with my pants down!" Moments later the towels I requested appeared under the stall. A few moments more and I emerged from the stall to see a somewhat shaken middle-aged man washing his hands; he saw me and immediately looked away mumbling an apology about my misfortune. My brother had never been in the bathroom; I had heard his laughing through the cold air return…

IN A GALAXY FAR, FAR AWAY...

I think there's something about virginity that just won't let it be concealed or disguised.

## MRS. SANTA'S SISTER

All I want for Christmas are some new front teats.

# ALVIN AND THE CHIPMUNK

I'm guessing he's at the store because he ran out of paper towel tubes. Because he cleans up after the gerbil a lot...get your mind out of the gutter.

Uhhh Roger, that's a big 10-4 on efficiency...

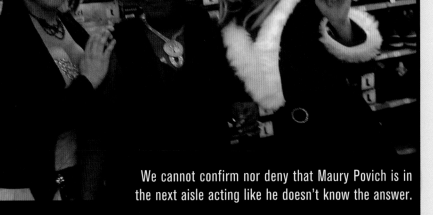

## TO WONG FOO, THANKS FOR EVERYTHING! JULIE NEWMAR

We cannot confirm nor deny that Maury Povich is in the next aisle acting like he doesn't know the answer.

You know, I was always ignoring and going against Jesus's wishes until I saw your homemade trench coat; then I was like, "Ohhh, okay, I'm supposed to do what he says. My bad."

WOOOOOOOOOOOO!

Styling and profiling huh? Boxes of inventory and fake plants…this hurts me so much.

UNKNOWN

Taking the term "backpack" a little lightly, aren't we?

Is that supposed to be figurative or literal? Because that's either funny and goofy or mean and rude.

ALABAMA

I guess you could say she had People of Walmart written all over her.

## YOU'RE NOT DOING IT RIGHT

Okay, let me break this down for you. Chronological order is an arrangement of events in the order of occurrence. In this case, you would buy the fishing rod and supplies, drive to your favorite fishing location, set up your equipment and get organized, and *then* you take your shirt off and relax...you'll get it.

FLORIDA

Once that creepy feeling leaves your spine, I would like to point out a few things that puzzled me. First, how is it the puppet is the better dresser? Second, do I spot a wedding ring? Because I think it would be awful being a ventriloquist's wife...I'll let your imagination figure out why.

## SITTIN' SIDEWAYS

There are only two ways to interpret this haircut. (1) An unnatural growth coming out of her head OR (2) She is wearing a mullet wig sideways. I prefer the latter.

## THE HOLY TRINITY

In the name of the father, son, and the holy Tweety bird?
That doesn't sound right, but I do love Looney Tunes!

## THE DARK SIDE

"I'm the Dark Angel"...No, you're the creepy girl who got made fun of growing up because she took longer than all the other girls to develop. But yeah, I guess your way of saying it is shorter.

## JUST BEAT IT

Yeah, I have a feeling that his palm generates enough friction to energize that whole suit.

**BLEACH BUM**

Bleach will just cause the black to fade! Just because you made license plates instead of doing laundry isn't an excuse! But I guess adjusting to life on the outside will have its bumps in the road.

**GOT MILK?**

Which gallon of milk do you think feels awkward and out of place, maybe even a little nervous depending on which state this is?

## TOUGH GUY

I wish I could up, up, down, down, left, right, B, A you in the face.

CANADA

Okay, okay, okay, serious question…would it be considered a foursome?

# WORKING HARD OR HARDLY WORKING

After work one night I had to stop at Walmart to pick up a few things. I was wearing khaki pants but was also wearing a hot pink, leopard-print hoodie and carrying a purse, as well as a shopping basket. (Yes, someone could have snapped a pic of me and submitted it.)

While doing my shopping, a little old lady approached me and asked me to help her find something. I politely told her that I did not work there and did not know where she could find what she was looking for. She walked away without saying anything, and I continued shopping. A few minutes later I hear someone saying, "That's her; she's the employee that was rude to me!" I turn to see the same little old lady pointing at me with a manager and looking very upset. The manager can see that I am not one of his employees and tries to explain this to the little old lady. "Nonsense!" she yells. "People wear khaki pants when they're at work so the customers will know that they work here." I went over to explain to the lady that I had just come from work to do some shopping. She *insisted* several times that the manager and I were in cahoots so that they wouldn't have to report me to corporate.

Finally, thinking she was playing along, she asked me where I *did* work and finally left me alone, or so I thought.

The next day I found out that she had called my work to complain to my boss that I was rude to her in Walmart.

Don't blame this kid for being smart enough to realize his dad is usually drunk enough to actually believe he is the police and fall for it.

**EYE SEE YOU**

Good thinking! Now you can see everyone giving you those disgusted looks behind your back.

**GOATS MAKE GREAT PETS!**

If you heard someone say out loud, "I'm going to put the goats in the back of my truck and go try to sell them in the Walmart parking lot" (1) Could you stop laughing? (2) Why are you married to your brother?

## BLOCK OUT THE BAD

Good thinking on the sunglasses, because the sun must have been directly in your eyes when you picked out that outfit.

UNKNOWN

## PIXAR PRESENTS...

Hey there, Lightning McQueen, why don't you try to go ahead and speed up your maturity to where you're too grown up to wear a *Cars* backpack?

## SHOWIN' SOME LOVE

I LOVE BLACK PEOPLE

F***in' a!

FLORIDA

## JUST CHECKIN' THE FRIDGE

I'm pretty sure he lives over in Aisle 5 and uses that as his personal refrigerator.

## BREAK ME OFF A PIECE

Create your own caption; I'm on the way to the hospital for a penicillin bath.

I think literally everyone in the world can agree with that, so I'm not sure if we really need it written out on a T-shirt.

## TRACK STAR

He's just finishing the world's longest track meet…
which started in 1977.

OHIO

## BUSINESS MODEL

Unfortunately once you buy that new cell phone you're gonna have to have your kids redraw you a bunch of new work shirts.

## PUT ME IN COACH

While we can all appreciate a good Bear Bryant tattoo, I'm just curious as to how you are now going to incorporate Nick Saban.

**CHILLIN' LIKE A VILLAIN**

Ever wonder what Prince would be like if he wasn't rich and famous?

# GET OFF MY LAWN!

I have to assume 85 percent of her day is consumed by sitting out in front of her apartment building smoking cigarettes and yelling at her tenants for being too loud and at kids for having fun.

## IT'S AMERICA'S TEAM ASSHOLE!

AMERICA'S TEAM! AMERICA'S STORE! A match made in heaven…or hell.

TEXAS

189

# WARM AND TOASTY

Sweet leg warmers! I guess it's a little chilly out there, huh Captain Kangaroo?

## ON THE CATWALK

Milk does a body F-A-B-U-L-O-U-S!!!!

## THE BIG RED MACHINE

If I don't assume that crib is either a gift for someone else or in some weird way for him, then I'm just gonna lose it because there is no way he can look after another human being.

NEW JERSEY

**NO CHILD LEFT BEHIND, JUST AN ASS**

You know that jackass who always takes up two parking spaces?

OHIO

## ...AND I'M ALSO A BAD PARENT

Hey Cheech, you do know Candy Land is just a game, right? There isn't any candy in there, and as awesome as it sounds, there really isn't a land made of candy. I hope she didn't space out and forget the baby.

# DUDE LOOKS (AND DRESSES) LIKE A LADY

Today I was in our local Walmart browsing around for cheap clothes. I was trying on a cute plaid button-up shirt and looking in one of those full-body mirrors they have around the clothing section when this older man comes up and starts browsing the women's clothes next to me. Take note: There was no child or woman with him. But anyway, there I was trying on this cute little shirt. By this time, this man is browsing through the same rack I am. I unbutton the shirt and take it off, placing it in my cart. I heard him say something, but I didn't know it was to me because he had been on the phone just moments before. But he says it again, louder, so I turn around. He says, "It looks very beautiful" and smiles very creepily at me. I mutter, "Thank you" and hurry away as quickly as I can, while returning the shirt to a nearby rack. What a stalker creep! Later I saw him looking at the little girl's clothes also...

## 2009 POWM HALL OF FAME INDUCTEE

It's official: We have our first PoWM Hall of Fame! This dude is cool as shit, and he always has a guaranteed spot on PoWM.

## HAPPY MEALS ON WHEELS

Ronald McDonald himself would be embarrassed and disappointed in this person.

## SANFORD AND SON

How do you pile that much crap that high? It looks like something from a cartoon!

## AQUA CAR

Seriously, are there no regulations regarding your vehicle? If you like boats so much, buy a damn boat. (And is that an article about your car-boat on your damn car-boat?)

## FARM LOVE

On that special day, nothing says "I love you" more than a Cow Limousine with a big piece of sh*t on the trunk (although rolling up to prom in this limo is actually a pretty sweet idea).

## TROLLIN' FOR FRIENDS

This doesn't scream "I'm lonely" at all…

# JURASSIC PARK

I'm not quite sure if Godzilla belongs on the dinosaur van, but since this guy included him, I'm glad he is at the very top where he belongs... Godzilla would beat down every other dinosaur. That's a fact. Look it up.

WEST VIRGINIA

# A MANICURIST'S DREAM OR NIGHTMARE?

So how does she wipe her ass??

# FOR BETTER OR WORSE

I can see they are at a photo hut. I see that. But what picture could be that important? NONE! Period. Don't bother telling me otherwise, because I'm not going to accept any answer other than Bigfoot and Nessie doing the Electric Slide.

# WALMART WEDDING

If you were wondering what this book is about, then here is your answer. This is the Holy Grail.

THE CROW

How is it that I'm scared to glance at the picture, but the older woman looks like she is ready to knock out that guy/girl/teenager that's angry at its parents?

I've got 4 to 1 odds saying she smelled her hand after she pulled it back out.

Cabbage Patch Man comes complete with a birth certificate and application for adoption. Each are sold separately.

## WORLD OF WALMART

He was just killing time while his supermodel girlfriend was shopping. I'm just kidding—his mom kicked him out of the basement to go make real friends because all he did was play World of Warcraft all day.

## NAIL FILED AWAY

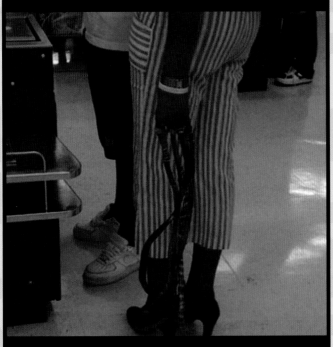

I should NEVER have to look twice at your hand to determine whether you are holding a few snakes or have really long fingernails.

I bet she is using like seventy-five Bumpits. And she looks like a hammer, which is pretty sweet.

## A HOT MESS

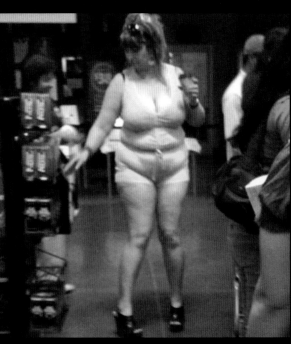

Do you think her and the rest of the music-hating Blue Meanies are gearing up for another attack on the Yellow Submarine?

Oh wow, that's neat, JanSport came out with a flesh-colored fanny pack...wait...wait a minute...hold on...that can't be... is it really?...OH MY DEAR GOD! Someone come and stab me in the neck so I'm distracted from this pain!

# I ONLY HAVE EYES FOR YOU

I am so disappointed in our entire human race right now. I'm angry at each and every one of you that we have gotten to this point as a species. I wish I could literally put every person in a timeout right now.

TEXAS

# ICE BATH

Back in my days of working at Walmart, on a disgustingly hot August day (98-degrees), a woman stormed up to the next register over. She demanded we refund the money that her husband had spent earlier that day when he purchased water.

My manager heard her screaming and came over. The customer went off on the manager explaining how she didn't waste money on water when she can get it from the tap, and it's our fault that the water was now all over the backseat of her car. The manager asked when the spouse had gotten the water, and she said he was here at 2:00 p.m.; he had left the items in the car while he ran other errands and got home at 6:30 p.m. That's when she found the water and came storming back to the store.

The manager took receipt and read it. He starts to say, "Ma'am, your husband purchased…" when she interrupts screaming, "My husband wanted to purchase ICE. The idiot here sold him WATER."

I never realized that people did not know that when ice is left to sit out in 98-degree weather it will melt and turn into water.

# ABOUT THE AUTHORS

Adam Kipple, Andrew Kipple, and Luke Wherry all grew up in the same town of Harrison City, Pennsylvania, located just outside Pittsburgh. Adam (25) is a web designer who graduated from the Art Institute of Pittsburgh and currently resides in Myrtle Beach, South Carolina, along with Luke (23), a graduate of the University of Pittsburgh. Andrew (24), a graduate of Xavier University, is currently in law school at Valparaiso University in Indiana.